APERTURE

APERTURE

poems by

PETER MAECK

illustrations by Alexandra Maeck

SHANTI ARTS PUBLISHING
BRUNSWICK, MAINE

APERTURE

Published by Shanti Arts Publishing
Designed by Shanti Arts Designs

Illustrations by Alexandra Maeck
and used with her permission.

"Adrift," "Despots," and "Black Site" were previously
published by *New Ohio Review*; "Testament" and
"Homage" were prevously published by *Unlikely Stories*.

Shanti Arts LLC
193 Hillside Road
Brunswick, Maine 04011
shantiarts.com

Printed in the United States of America

ISBN: 978-1-956056-58-7 (softcover)

Library of Congress Control Number: 2022943823

for Jessie

Contents

ƒ/2

Aperture	12
Pyre	13
My Captain	14
Upriver	16
Interstice	18
Blessing	21
Specimen	23
Haven	25
Vulcan	26
Adrift	29
Testament	30
Badge	32
Lauterbrunnen	34
Quarry	36
Diadem	37
The Slug	38

ƒ/4

Homage	42
Anchorite	44
Tailings	46
Diviners	49
Korengal	52
Debrief	53
Supplicant	56
Moirai	58
Apologia	60
Audition	62
Diddly	64
Felon	66
Despots	68
Black Site	71
Potlatch	73

ƒ/8

Hegira	86
Conjugation	88
Songbird	90
Collateral	92
Entente	94
Prime Mover	95
Stasi	96
The Proud and Randy Fellows	98
Guest Services Directory	100

ƒ/16

Lost At Sea	106
Laureate	107
Feedlot	108
Misfit	109
Obloquy	110
Coup	112
The End of the Affair	114
Next Door	115
Euphonium	117

ƒ/32

In Common	122
Child's Play	123
Pyramid Scheme	124
Tempus Fugitaboudit	125
FAQ	126
Baited/Switched	127
Credo	128
Same Difference	129
Apt Pupil	130
Skill Set	131
American League Champions	132
All My Loving	133

ƒ/64

Ontogeny	136
Blank Verse Blank	137
About the Author and Contributor	139

f/2

Aperture

In this album are all of my pictures
Of all of the gliders I've flown;
Of all of the shrines where I've whispered in vain;
Of all of the shoes that I own.
I have, though, no views of rooms I've abandoned;
Nor of birds that have flown.

My shutter, it seems, will not open
On things that are no longer true.
And sadder than that, my depth of field
Has shallowed; now my view
Is glaucomatous. I can't tell you for love
Or for money what's borrowed, what's blue;
Nor old, nor new.

Who are you? That is my question.
I mean as distinguished from me.
Or say, as distinguished from the punk
Of this beetle-bored tree?
Answer quickly,
It's late and we're losing the light
Degree by degree.

You don't want your picture taken.
Truth told, few of us do.
We'd rather remain unmounted, unframed,
Uncaptured, unexposed,
Out of view.
Your picture will join all of those I've not taken
Of many before, now of you.

Pyre

The house is ash and embers, nothing to reclaim
That I can see,
Unless this china plate and cup set as for tea.
As well, perhaps this metal crutch: the man was lame.
I did not know him well. Somehow
I never waved nor called. Well, not now.

He was a teacher, of some science, did research,
Somewhere far north, collected stones,
Assigned them ages. Was not a member of our church,
Was not beloved by those for whom he did his work,
Those matriculants all drowsing, drowning in his stones,
His knotty, tangled talk. Their hooded eye,
Their smirk.

Why stones? Such things so dark and mute.
Of Pliny, Dante, Augustine I would perorate
Were I what I am not: the teaching sort;
Were I this man whom I knew not,
Whose house is burnt.

Whose stones, however, now appearing
In the sudden streetlamp light,
Studded in the soot gem-like,
Are Cygnus, Ursa Major, Virgo just as if
This sodden, reeking char
Were starry night.

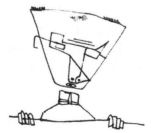

My Captain

A parrot come at Surabaya,
Come aboard the ship,
Alight on deck.
My captain take the parrot
In his cabin, feed it, watch it sleep,
He say that it remind him of his
Dear dead wife, the way it talk,
The color of her head.

The company regulation say:
Don't Keep a Parrot On the Ship.
My captain tell the company what
The reason why he keep the parrot.
He say yes I know the regulation.
Save for this one I obey all regulation.
Regulation in my book be holy writ.
That said, the week now that I keep
The parrot, feed it, watch it sleep,
It be the gladdest week since
My dear wife be dead.

The company write back, say:
Don't Keep a Parrot On the Ship.
And so my captain strangle it.

Next day my captain strip
His cabin, throw out carpet,
Table, desk, the bed, the books.
A rocking chair, a naked bulb,
A radio is all he keep. I walk in,
See him rocking in the naked light,

He tapping out Black Sabbath
On the radio with the big toe
Of his two bare feet.

This captain be the one who
Few weeks after that laid course
Against the downbound traffic
In the Persian Gulf. You saw
The paper so you know how
That turn out.

Upriver

We try to leave New York just after lunch
so we'll make Hanover by dark in time
to view the campus green aflame
in sunset light.
I want to take Route 5 along the riverbank
so he can see what I saw at his age
on my first trip. But he is slow
to pack and so we're not away
'til six but that's all right, we're
on the road, my brand-new Escalade,
fit with custom shocks just gobbling up the
Interstate. The feeling's less like driving
than it is like soaring in a glider up on thermals,
all my sense of speed and place is lost.
You know, I say to him, when I was young
there was no Interstate.
(I'm Class of '48.)
He's balled his sweater up into a pillow
for his head against the window.
Yes, I rode the bus up old Route 5,
through all the towns,
the forests, and the luncheonettes.
The farther north you went the
more you felt the games of Murder
in the Dark, the blues you caught,
those summers out at Orient Point,
the kiss that left the taste of
Starburst in your mouth,
evaporate.
There's something I forgot, he blurts.
I'll mail it, Jack.
Can't wait, Dad.
Hey, relax, I'll send it overnight.
(Poor kid, he wishes I'd turn back.)

He's silent after that. His face
reflecting the phosphorescence
of the dash's instruments,
his lips are fluffing as the breath flows
in and out. I see our exit up ahead.
Ah, no, just Windsor, good, I wasn't ready yet.
Jack mutters in his sleep and I accelerate
into the vastness of this night, beneath
the Archer and the Arrow toward this
dauntless river's ice-fed and pellucid source
four hundred miles above its mouth
between Old Saybrook and Old Lyme
where, silted and sludge-choked,
its freshness turned to salt, it terminates.

Interstice

When in the womb you're rather small,
But pre-conceived you're not at all.

You're neither head nor arm nor leg.
You're not a sperm, you're not an egg.

You're nada, zippo, diddly, zero;
Nobody's fool and nobody's hero.

No one has loved you; you've never been kissed.
The world could care less that you don't yet exist.

On the other hand, though, and I'm not being funny,
You're free of all guilt and you owe no one money.

But while that's the case, the converse is true:
You owe not a penny, but none's owed to you.

Maybe you're better off not being born,
Safe in the dark, never seeing the morn.

Consider the limbo before you drew breath:
Is the state before birth any different from death?

If it isn't then you must admit that the tomb
Doesn't differ in function or form from the womb.

It is just one more green room where actors await
The calls to their places, the cues to their fate.

Your life goes in cycles; death makes a loop, too.
Or not—maybe death sticks around just like glue,

And your life is a candle whose all too brief flicker
Flicks off when angina takes hold of your ticker.

Who knows? No one can 'cause it's out of our ken.
Your guess will be errant ten times out of ten.

But hey, it's all foolishness, who gives a hoot
What happens without us? The question is moot,

Just as wondering: *Hm, does a tree make a sound
If there's no one to hear when it falls to the ground?*

And yet we do wonder, we can't check our yearning
To answer the questions so urgent, so burning:

What happens before us? And then when we die?
Do our lives have more meaning than that of a fly?

Was the world dark without us, no moon in the sky
When we were just glints in our parents' left eye?

Did Mom and Dad plan us? Or leave us to luck
The night that the two of them lay down to pluck

Up the courage to say, "Love, our youth has now fled.
It's time to be parents, so let's off to bed?"

Imagining parents conjoining this way
Is harder than holding your breath for a day,

More painful than peeling the skin from a blister,
Less fun than the notion of kissing your sister.

We'd rather believe we were brought by the stork
Than admit that we started when Dad popped his cork.

Conception immaculate—hey, that term pleases.
We're children of God, the siblings of Jesus.

Wearing our halos on top of our head,
Immortal like He who arose from the dead.

I speak not as one whom the Word of God moves;
I don't grant a devil with pitchfork and hooves.

Alas, I'm not Christian, nor Muslim, nor Buddhist.
To tell me to pray is like telling a nudist,

"Hey, pull up your pants!" or "Your fly is wide open!"
It's oxymoronic, yet most folks are hopin'

The soul never dies, that it flies like a dove
Not to hell but straight upward to heaven above.

I confess that I doubt the existence of Satan;
It's not in my plans to be soon Pearly Gatin'.

'Cause heavenly rest isn't what I most covet.
(Though plenty of people do swear that I'd love it.)

It's life here on earth that I most want to last;
I favor the present o'er future and past.

I don't scorn the future, nor hate long ago.
It's just that the present is all that I know.

Blessing

I spoke in tongues a night in early March
with bleating voices all about,
a microphone held dagger-like
to my throat.
I'd happened in by accident.
I'd seen the light, heard the bleating voices
through the painted windows,
heard the pastor shout.
Inside, deep in a corner at the back
I stood politely crouched,
unseen I thought, astonished by
the blare of metal instruments, the leaping,
sheening congregants, the cloud of sweat
like smoke, the seismic quaking
of the pine boards underfoot.
You there! A hand upon my wrist.
What? No.
Step forth!
I'm pulled from subtle dimness into
blasting, bobbleheaded, brawling
light. Excuse me! Wait! I shout,
though not a word comes out.
(My tongue's stuck to the dry roof
of my mouth.)
I'm not the man you want!
Bless us!
How? With what?
You have been chosen! Speak!
I have no voice!
Which is the truth although the amps
make thunder of my pulse; make
gale wind of my addled breath.
Folks, wait a sec, I am not,
as you all seem to think,
a man of your own faith.

He speaks!
No, I did not.
What's that? Louder now! Speak up!
The mic is pushed against my lips,
I taste the pastor's spit. Now to an overwhelming
question I've been led: To sputter hooey off the
top part of my head (as if possessed), or stay mute
and thus the faithful disappoint.
Er, ah, um, I blurt.
He is risen! all my new friends shout.
Then they, reclaiming coats, file out;
the blistered players meanwhile
packing up their instruments.
For years thereafter I don't give a thought
to the event but then it all returns
dreamlike. So I take pen and write:
Remember me? The One Who Spoke?
The postman takes the letter,
brings it back within a week:
NO KNOWN ADDRESS RETURN TO SENDER
I would phone my erstwhile fellow congregants
if I had their number but at this point what in
God's name would I say to them in any case?
Plus, I lost my voice the very night I waxed
so eloquent. But never mind, I've said enough
and anyway, I've found that silence is
the long-lost, long-sought key to blessed,
dreamless sleep from which, if you were
granted just one wish, you'd wish
not ever to awake.

Specimen

I find him
here upon the
Oriental, on his back, his knees
upraised, his legs thus in an A-shape.
Tripped and fell, he says. Damn
rug, it's curling at the edge.
It is indeed, I note.
He can't get up,
He who gave me noon and night
and morning this advice:
Do not, for hell or heaven's
sake, capitulate.
Capitulate? To what? I said.
He shook his head. Had I not seen
the words he'd penciled on the
flyleaves of my Golden Books?
You know of what I speak, he said.
(And yes, I did.)
I reach to lift him up.
Dead weight.
He pulls free of my grip.
I'm not an invalid, he hisses,
'least not yet.

In dreams I am a monarch
in a jar with cotton balls
suffused with ethyl acetate.
Awaking, I remark upon
my thorax skewered
with a silver spike, my wings
pinned back. My name in Latin's
on the card just to my right,
block-printed by some
junior high school lepidopterist.
I am a sort of Gregor Samsa,

or would be if, like he,
I could still perambulate.
But me, I'm stuck.
I do not, though, bemoan
or curse my fate.
So many if not most throughout
the annals of recorded time
have suffered worse.
He, for instance,
on the carpet at my feet.
I ask him, Shall I fill a chalice
at the tap? Would a wafer
give you strength to resurrect?
My tone is mocking which tomorrow
or next week I will regret,
but which in light of our positions
after eons switched
is apt.

I must be off. I have so many
broken promises to keep.
And so goodnight sweet prince
of darkness who of late
held high for millions,
or for me at least, the lamp
of everlasting light.

Haven

Just think
when they were young
they might have shinnied
knee-and-ankle-barking up the
scabrous oak; caught spiders
deep within the dented,
dripping water spout;
set course to where the sky
meets earth where there be dragons,
it once was thought.
Were there dragons? They'd find out.
But they remained within the confines
of the holy day instead,
mindful of the sacred hour,
fetal at the rail, tongue out
through lips pursed guppy-like
to taste the host: corpus delicti
of another sort.
Just think,
unless perhaps you'd rather not,
of what they missed,
these star-blessed or Lord God
forbid star-cursed communicants,
young lovers of the Eucharist,
their troubles, they believed, so few.
Youth
so brave and true
is wasted on the young
as it was not,
as you are bold to say,
on such as you.

Vulcan

We quake the moment
we're assigned a job
to do it's not that we're
incompetent it's just that
we can't concentrate since
we had our had our had
our accident (a head-
on wreck, a booby-
trapped device, or we were
raped, what difference
does it make?)
which left us in this slightly, no,
not slightly, more than slightly
altered state. And so it goes
like this: we take
an order then we just
forget it when we're halfway
to the place where we're to
do the work, and then ashamed to be
our futile self we turn around and slink
back to the man in
charge to ask just what
the order was. He rolls
his eyes like huh what are you
some cross-
bred mis-
born half-
wit can't keep a simple order
in your head? We chuckle like
you're right so get a Mensa brainiac, we quit.
We don't say that, though, instead,
we try once more to
get it right, repeating in our head
the order so that this time we'll remember it.

Nine times out of ten
that does the trick but every tenth
time we go blank.
That's the nightmare, going blank, losing all
our sense of time and place. Where are we?
Did we volunteer? Who signed us up?
Or are we dreaming? Damn that's hot,
the ingot, or the pizza slice, or some electrified
and shorted-out component part we wrap it,
set it in the box, and now
it has our fingerprints unless
our fingerprints burned off, our hands
are shaking and our breath
is coming fast and short.
We have to pee now from the Mickey's
Malt we drank, then we chased it with an aquavit
and meanwhile all the others working, working,
whistling while they work, while we're
at sea, adrift, about to weep. The feeling now
arrives, on cue, the feeling in our
private parts. We try to stop it but we can't.
The more we try the worse, the worse, it gets.
The weird thing is that while it's getting
worse we're feeling like a million bucks,
now figure that one out.
We'd love this feeling any other time,
we'd wallow in it, we'd luxuriate but
now is not the time for that
to say the least. Our heart
is crashing through our chest,
our eyes are hot with blood, our skin is
sizzling now our gums begin to hurt
because our teeth are clenched so tight. We start
to howl, not with our voice,
just in our head, a wolf,

the woods all black, we wonder
if the wolf is happy, sad, or just amazed
to see the moon above which when we were
a kid we thought was a projector
lamp, the film had stuck, the frame that was
a view of Delft had melted into brickle
shapes and then the screen went bleaching,
blinding white.
The scene now shifts to
Vulcan or some iron-forging fellow
of his type, his hands inside
asbestos gloves, his bellows blowing coals
red hot, his hammer clanging, steel
like taffy, dunk it in the water, poof
it's cool, the Golden Spike, it hurts
to death, the Wedding of the Rails.
Oh God please
make us stop, we've made our point.
Too late, the whistle now
it's time to quit, the stars come out,
the ring around the moon,
beneath our back the lake with ice
so thick it holds a horse but not a cart,
it cracks with a report just like
a pistol shot, the cart falls
through and sinks, we fall
asleep headfirst the bubbles intermixed
with silt rise up, we wake, the blacksmith doesn't
find us, wouldn't find us
if he looked.
I do, I do, I do
until our death shall do us part
unless, by blessed accident,
the dead one isn't me;
instead: my heart.

Adrift

The year we were a State Farm agent
we would rather now forget.
We hated scaring folks: Imagine that
your house incinerates or God forbid
you're stricken with a fatal this or that
(it could be symptomless) or there's
a workplace accident, you're dis-
membered then what happens to
your spouse and kids? They're up
the so-called creek.

Adrift, we turned to animal husbandry but we wept
to slaughter pigs; we planted beets but with the drought
we just gave up the naïve hope of ever making
gentleman farming work. We entered politics
sometime after that ran for a City Council seat,
lost in a rout. We drowned ourself in drink.
Our spouse absconded with Meg and Mike
the twins and sued us for divorce.

Depressed, to say the least,
we drove out on a ferry boat, the one that goes from
Boxport out to Riley's Point. We gunned it, shot
straight out the other end, right through the safety
chain, think Thelma and Louise. Our canyon, though,
was harbor water, sludgy, twelve feet deep. We didn't die,
they pulled us out. The Camry was a total loss,
of course, the motor's scrap once salt gets in it.
Stupid the attempt to drown ourself
in shallow water, better odds
out farther in the rip.
The blues run there, we caught one
at the age of six, in our father's
Boston Whaler, never had a
better day than that one since.
One day a life can make.

Testament

I did not disappoint.
Your present lives are better now
than what they were before me
to the tune of eighty-six percent.
My misdeeds, if you'd even call them misdeeds,
more like minor lapses which in time will seem
like gallant leaps of faith, were mild
and were committed with
the purest of intent.
I get teary-eyed now thinking back:
Our torch-lit midnight cavalcades
of mustering consent;
the thousand skeptics flailing
in the semi-frozen quarry mud.
Last rites!
The yowling bonfires on those
wind-burned, snow-blind,
pyromanic nights!
Our profaners bridled,
fettered, trussed while
we their last-born roasted
plum pits in the bleacher seats!
(Ah, youth.)
Those were the days, my friends,
not ever, so we thought,
to be cut short.
They were the best days
of our flimsy lives,
you must on pain of painful
this or that admit.
All right, the pain, if pain
we call it, now is mine in fact,
or will be at the moment
I'm suspended mid-air
by this hawser 'round my neck:

your gaping marionette.
It is to you
my fairest weather suppliants
that I this farewell carol dedicate.
Now this final note:
I die intestate.
That is, no doubt, a shock to all my
self-presumptive heirs and assigns
with their seats booked for the reading
of my last and latest will and testament.
Really, though, dear kids,
once you had lost your faith,
what else did you expect?
This hurts me more than you
since, as you know, I hate
to disappoint, but honestly
what right have you to disappointment
when I've cast you in the choicest roles and
placed you on the brightest stage whereon
to strut and fret the scant remainder your
little lives, star-turning every
ten or fifteen minutes in the
greatest show on earth?
And so forth.
Hangman, butcher, baker,
do your worst.

Badge

I'm leaving for awhile to win the day.
Last night I heard the bugle call;
today I hear the fife, the drum.

I'll be away a month, or two.
Less than that I could not do
what needs be done to bring
the proof to everyone.

I will return enwreathed, beribboned,
with an emblem studding the lapel
of my lieutenant's coat: the badge
hand-wrought of precious tin
worn just by those who lose
less than they win.

I have applauded 'til my palms bled
each year's crop of inductees into
the House of High Repute.
Now, to put it bluntly, it is time
I wore the hallowed silver lamé suit.

Unless, of course, I'm back in theory
only, not in flesh. In that case
post your accolades by
transmundane express.

I know, how can I joke when facing
all but certain loss of limb, or knock
on solid oak, some torment
worse than death?

It is because where there is laughter
there is sempiternal life, as goes

the motto on the flyleaf of my
general issue writ which is
so thick and hard with truth that it
would stop a bullet speeding to my heart
before it even reached page thirty-six.

Well, I'm off. No tears, pretend
I've just ducked out for cigarettes.
In parting, this: If I do not return
just when I said I would, don't fret.
The chances are I'm stuck in
traffic at the bridge, or else my
flight was scrubbed. Please
don't imagine that I'm
headless in a ditch.
Don't think that I've been captured
and that under physical duress
I've hawked up all your passcodes
and divulged your home address.
More likely I have simply dawdled
on their side for just a bit;
swooned, as 'twere, in their green
valleys where the lapwings soar
in mists of tulip scent. Or I met
and wed someone of their profane
persuasion and their grotesquely
misproportioned look.
Do you think I would do that?
For if I did then you could
call me recreant. You could say
I had the damned cheek to defect.
And for all of that, you would be right,
now come to think.

Lauterbrunnen

If you were I,
or better put, if I,
let's say, were you,
I would ascend along
the Weisse Lütschine, passing
Wilderswil on the Grenshenstrasse,
onward then to Lauterbrunnen
there to stand before the Staubbachfall;
there to glorify the Eiger and the Jungfrau
and the Mönch.

But if you did this,
I have fear that you, no less than I,
would see the beau ideal of time and place that
you had conjured in your waking dreams
and your perfervid sleep now convolute,
collapse, and transubstantiate to just
a few dark-star convergence points,
unseen in fulgent day, now feebly glinting,
soon to vanish in the gelid night.

Buck up, you say.
Yes, yes, you're right. But when I had your age
my eye was bright, until that snowblind moment
when my reds and blues and greens
devolved to gray and white.
Your age, I say as if we were so far apart,
as if we didn't share a birthday, hadn't ever traded
baseball cards, hadn't split a bottle of Prosecco,
did not in equal measure love our wife.

But yes, why don't I just take in whatever's
there to take, and not reflect, as you would do
if you stood where I stand,
or at worst a little to my left
or right, or sat upon my shoulders,
or stood atop my head?

But you can't, or won't, and by the time you do
I'll be ascending along the Weisse Lütschine,
passing Wilderswil, pressing on to Lauterbrunnen,
there to fall before the Staubbachfall, struck dead
by those who thought that I was you, not knowing
I'd been paid whatever was the going rate to take
your place in line right up there near the head
to fight for gods and countries
in your stead.

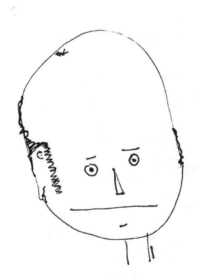

Quarry

There are no atheists in foxholes,
the vixen said,
no ski lift attendants, no batboys
for the Cincinnati Reds.

There are no atheists in foxholes,
the foxhounds agreed,
And they would know, they are
the fox-hunting breed.

There are no atheists in demand as CPAC speakers,
which goes without saying;
none even who in hopes of getting the gig
mime praying.

There are no atheists tithing a tenth of their wages,
or even a nickel,
which doesn't mean they wave the red flag with the gold star above
the hammer and sickle.

There are no atheists baptizing their babies
with holy water,
but very many love both Schubert's
and Pergolesi's Stabat Mater,

and have no trouble loving Sikhs, Jews,
and Episcopalians,
and don't dismiss creationists out of hand as
extraplanetary aliens;

and, when gone to ground, the pack halted by the whippers-in
and the huntsman's horn, are flushed to guns, the blooding
of the youngest rider's cheek announcing
yet another hunter born.

Diadem

We would have madly loved them had it only been
a Saturday.
And you'd have, too, we're sure, in March or May,
or in the cruelest month, the one between.
Imagine then the sound of carillons,
the velvet evenings and the rosy-fingered dawns,
had their eyes been blue instead of gray, or green.

Our children would have met and played;
some might have wed.
As is, they've not so much as shaken hands, nor broken bread.
Their parents' debt to us remains unpaid,
their mortal flesh and immortal souls unshriven.
All would have been forgiven
had they not disdained the one to whom we prayed.

The fault, it must be said, is not with them;
it's in their seed.
They are, all due respect, a churlish breed
unlike ourselves; not born to wear the diadem;
writing with the wrong hand, when they write at all,
a crabbed, back-slanting scrawl.
Mind you, we do not denigrate, nor condemn.

But we have wasted too much time
with them in bed.
Truth told, they weren't that good. That said,
what fools we were in making them our concubine.
Well, lesson learned.
The bed's been burned,
the sheets are washed and bleached and hanging on the line,
the old bottles, drained of dregs, await new wine.

The Slug

Would you take one hundred dollars to consume this slug?
You shake your head. How about I add a Persian rug?
I'll even throw in first-class airfare to and from Khartoum.
You're not all in?
Consuming slugs, you say, is both unhealthy and a sin?
Forbidden philosophically by David Hume?
Toxic to whatever's forming up inside the mother's womb?
Ach! Such gloom and doom!

Five hundred, fine, and not a penny more.
And the rug, of course.
And yes, the trip to Sudan's still included, plus an Appaloosa horse.
That's all I've got, I cannot offer more.
You'll eat it, then? Alive?
How much d'you want to gobble five?
No, wait, ten grand is yours if you ingest a score!
You ask, what for?
Why am I so keen on making you a culinary whore?
Is the slug per se important? Or is it what the slug stands for?
So many questions. What a bore.

No, the slug is not important, nor the other stuff.
It could be anything that tempted you
to do some vile or awkward thing you thought you'd never do,
like attending Sunday service in the buff,
then at the altar rail
complaining that the wine is swill and the wafer stale.
For such embarrassment would my love be recompense enough?
(Albeit any love I gave you would be very tough.)
Would you take two keys of fine grade eucalyptus snuff?
A Ritz-sized diamond in the rough?
One ton gross weight of French marshmallow fluff?

Good! You agree! On condition I explain the purpose of the game.
Well, if I tell you there is none,
and that it's just for fun
I would be lying 'cause the purpose is to shame
the one who takes the loot;
who wolfs down, so to speak, the once-forbidden fruit
in Mammon's or in any other graven, golden idol's name.

Au contraire is your reply;
in self-humiliation there's no shame;
there's only courage; thereby fame.
The hero is proud to suffer embarrassment; is glad to die;
will eat the slug and then post hoc
will welcome septic shock,
and in a granite mausoleum will forever after lie.

In light of that you now say *you'll* pay *me* to eat the slug,
for just a dime,
which, as you're a little short right now, you'll remit over time.
I say nuts to that, unless for prophylaxis I could take a sulfa drug.
No? Why not? 'Cause then I'd be a cheat?
I have to take the critter neat
if I want all those pretty Mary Magdalenes to wash my feet?
Well, put like that I'm forced to say your deal is sweet.
Already I hear praises sung by each of my idolators
upon his prayer rug;
I see my haloed head and name in gold leaf on your coffee mug;
Stop me if I'm sounding too presumptuous, or smug.
And if you can't afford the dime, I'll take a hug.
But if you won't embrace the kind of thug
Who'd trick you into suicide-by-slug,
Then promise me you'll bless my soul
As you lay me in the hole that you've just dug.

f/4

Homage

We are flooded
to our necks. Like fishing bobbers
we are floating on our backs down what,
before the storm, was Maple Street.
Full fathom five now is our neighborhood
and all that shows above the ever-rising
bilge and brine are chimney tops.
Three cheers! This ends the drought
and we say thanks for that and for
our lives which you have saved while
that of all the others in this
wanton city you have not.

We are burning
up. The drought is back, six years
without a drop. There's not the moisture
in our mouths to even spit. The woods
ignite with every lightning bolt.
Stubbled char is now where green-
and yellow-tasseled head-high
corn once stood. Ah well, we never
fancied lumbering or farming much
and now you've saved us from such work
and soon, you say, you'll bless us with
an unemployment check.

We are strong
against the bane since
we are older but we stand
here helpless, hearts rent,
mouth agape all while it ravages
our kids. What is their guilt?
What did they do to so incense you, sir?
Of decency, I ask you, have you not
an atom left?

Now (and thank you very much)
we are concussed, our cheekbone
cracked, our upper right incisor
gone. (We think we swallowed it,
our tongue now probes the gap.)
You tell us in your viscous, worldly
famous crooner's voice that we have
thus received of you your greatest gift:
your kiss.

We would kiss you
back except that you're so, how to say,
so statuesque compared to us down
in the dirt that even standing tippy-toe
and reaching to the sky we'd never touch
your lips and so as per the ancient rite
we kiss your bootblacked hobnailed feet.

Anchorite

I beseech thee Lord to make me chaste,
But not just yet.
I'd like to finish first my buttered warm baguette
Which would be, of course, a crime to waste,
As would my *café noir.*
And may I have your kind permission to repair to the pissoir?

Almighty Father, if it be your will,
I'd love a date
With either Pippa or her sister Princess Kate.
Please also have my local CVS refill
My Oxycodone and my Fentanyl.
Of both I'm down to one last pill.

Once you've done all this then I'll be glad
To cease to be an infidel.
I'll give up sex as well,
Or give up sex at least that's undertaken while unclad,
'Cause who calls sex between consenting partners
Wearing hazmat suits
Bad?
You do?
Darn it. Well, then I must, too.

Saint Augustine, of course, inspires me
To lose what I most covet;
To sneer at carnal lust and rise above it.
A slave to God is all I want to be.
Seventy-two virgins, no, make that seventy-three
Will be my modest fee.
What? Save one for you?

You didn't say that, God. No, that didn't sound like you.
But if you did then you're not God in which case
Who in God's name
Am I talking to?
Oh, no. It's not. Don't tell me, please don't tell me
That it's you.
'Cause then I'm through.

Tailings

Look at you,
tagged out one foot short of
second base inside the old abandoned
ballpark where the dead-and-gone-to-hell-
or-heaven minor leaguers used to play,
not one in fifty thousand ever rising
out of Double-A. (No wonder since
their hardball skills were better
suited to croquet.)

They caught you stealing,
which when added to the batter's strikeout
ended up an inning-ending double-play
that ruined what was otherwise
a grand Old Timers' Day.
Well, now you have to pay.
Thou Shalt Not Steal Thy Neighbor's
Second Base, at least not on
the Sabbath Day.

Look at you,
between the creamery and the foundry
in the alleyway face down upon the
lemon rinds and carrot shavings
tossed from upper-story windows
by the cooks who simply couldn't wait
for garbage pickup day, and now
the chapel choir sings Hallelujah
as your lifeblood seeps away.

Look at me,
all primped and plumped, tail wagging,
'cause I thought I'd flunked the final
but I got an A.
Say hey!

You are invited to my wedding. Yes,
I'm getting married in the morning
once I choose between my curly
and my straight-haired fiancée.
(Our little wee one is already
on the way.)
Look at me,
my Purple Heart, my Bronze Star,
and my Oak Leaf Cluster that I won
for sacrificing arm and leg in service
to the Mother of All Exiles in the
Battle of Sayyd Alma Kalay.

How did our yellow-wooded roads
diverge in such a way, when both
that morning equally lay, and we
were as one traveler thinking
we could take the first and keep
the other for another day?

We flipped a coin for who'd go left
and who'd go right but the nickel landed
edgewise and though we huffed and
puffed to knock it over that's where clearly
it was going to stay.

We drew straws but both were short.
We wet our fingers, raised them high:
I would brave the gale while you
would ride a zephyr to a lemon sky
and thus, just as I'd planned it,
you would live and I would die.
But you were wise to me and wouldn't play.

You wouldn't let me sacrifice my life so you
could live and love another day. You shied
from wealth and fame, you spit the bit.
You made your bed and peed and shat in it
and ever since you've been content
to lie in it while I'm condemned to
suffer in my hacienda with my vineyards,
polo ponies, Tesla, and survivor's guilt.
Well, thanks for nothing,
and you're welcome
while I think of it.

Diviners

Water we will find with our forked stick!
they advertised.
As if the water were metal, and the implement magnetized.
It is solid science how it works, not a trick as is
transmuting water into wine.
Our work will seem miraculous; you will think that we
are heaven-sent.
Please don't. We are diviners by profession but,
we must be frank,
are not ourselves divine.

We hired them on the spot.
We had no choice. After what was now six years of drought
our fields were dust, our well dry, leaving us to doubt
what God in his professed beneficence had wrought.
Behold our once forever rolling amber waves of grain
now withered into mange-patched stubbled tracts for lack of rain.

Pay us half upfront, they said, the balance when, not if
we get results.
We balked. *Relax*, they said, you *think that*
we are shamans from a voodoo cult? Honestly,
you're acting more like children
than mature adults.

Shamed, we ponied up.

They got to work, each diviner with the twin tines
of his stick held at a level just below the belt
so that the single prong poked straight ahead.
In consequence they looked liked they'd unzipped
and whipped their Sir Johns out to urinate.
Ha-ha, we said.

The bottle rocket of the sun arising on the left
now burst and glitter-showered back down on the right.
No water yet discovered, the diviners bedded down
on thorns and thistles for the night.

No luck was theirs the next day nor the next
day after that.
Their sticks refused to twitch. Instead of water
only twenty dozen ancient Roman coins
turned up whose current total value,
we surmised, was less than fifty cents,
and in the meantime we stayed cotton-mouthed.

My thirst-crazed wife ran to the beach.
Water, water everywhere! she cried,
and filling up her chalice, took a long cool drink,
and minutes later floated out toward open ocean belly-up.

She'd forgotten that before one sips the sea
one must desalinate. This costs, however, much
too much, for us at least, and what to do with all
that salt?

And so our only hope at this dire point was finding
water fresh and sweet that ran through caverns
dark and measureless to man far down
beneath our feet.

But none was found and when the days
became a week our soi-disant diviners
just gave up.
Thanks for nothing, mountebanks, we said.
We want our money back.

Too late, they said, *we've sent it home*
to help our families homeless in
tsunami's wake.
We shouted: *See you then in court!*
We sued but then their sharkskinned
lawyer got the case thrown out.

So now we lie here, we the group's surviving
ten percent, without the moisture on our tongues
to spit, gaming out our final days with
Caesar's golden quarter, Pompey's silver dime,
And Diocletian's copper nickel as our tiddlywinks.

If precious metal slaked our thirst
then we would not bemoan
that water no more seeps from coins
than blood flows from a stone.

Korengal

Home
from Korengal I got a hunch my whole head's
not on tight or either that or else it's on too tight depends
on day or night today mistook my sister for a hat I
dreamed that I was tied up hands and feet and shot

Home
I wonder why in hell ten months in Korengal I didn't die for
god and country took a round right in the eyeball while the
IED near halved the other guy

Home
now I'm the local hero mister freakin' saint they put my name
on my old school my name is now the name of my old street
no thank you folks just dunk me in a tub of printer's ink
the color black is all I need for my war paint

Home
the neighbor says stop screaming in your sleep I tell her
fourth and goal my captain calls a bombing run it's stuffed
he shoulda called a passing play by play O say the rockets
or the ramparts glaring Hulu streaming stripes and tracers
broadly gleaming what so proudly oh my dear the bombs
are bursting loud and clear inside my deafened inner ear

Home
sweet home is where the heart is but I left my heart in
Korengal damn thing just won't come back I better go
and get it better finish what I started 'cause a
Christian soldier can't be running from a fight
I tell you what though to my everliving shame
give me the choice I wouldn't swat a fly
(no foul no crime)
I'd be a Jain
and that's just what I'll be next time

Debrief

Where was I
when you achieved the world's first
circumnavigation of a gibbous moon
hands cuffed behind your back and
wearing leg weights? (Oh, your
prowess makes me swoon.)

Where was I
when my battalion down
to fifteen men withstood the
deathly libels launched from drones
not more than six feet overhead?
(Don't think that I was home in bed.)

Where was I
when you accused me (wrongly)
of declaring in the town square that
I wished you dead?

I'll tell you where I was if I could
get a word in edgewise:

I was here
where I was not
yet thought myself to be,
my thoughts as nothing
vis-à-vis your immaculate decree.

I was here
when history stopped and those
condemned to learn from it
misremembered, rinsed, and then
repeated it.

I was here
and there and everywhere
to lead a better life I am denying there
is anyone besides the one who's now,
was then, and always will be there
and thus I know, or dearly hope at least,
that I need never care.

I was here
at the chastening of the last remaining
recreants. I'd walked the nine miles from
my home. by the tourmaline caves, through
the goblin forest, across the lacquer of the
wintered lake, afraid of not arriving on the dot
since those arriving late, we'd all been warned,
would face a hefty fine and no-shows
would be shot. It was so lovely of you
after the event to invite us all to gorge
on ortolan and angel cake.

Now having said all this I'd say that
you should let me live another day.
I'd say that would be fair,
as otherwise my only hope is that
you'll find it in your cold black heart
to grant me three or two or why be
greedy just one single final breath of air.

'Cause ain't it rich—of course I'm
paraphrasing—you and me a pair?
Me in the end with my head in a
storm drain and you in your
hot-air balloon in mid-air.

You'll pay for what you do to me,
my friends know where you live.
You think I'm kidding? I'm sincere.
They used to tremble when you
called them up for coffee, now
they have no fear. They'll get you
first thing in the morning, or just after
lunch, or maybe if they're running late,
next year.

Supplicant

You bring us landfill in a demitasse.
It smells of arrogance.
It smacks of teen romance.
It isn't even made of brass.
We pass.
Feel free, though, to return if
You invent a non-invasive strain
Of social class.

Re: This patent you submit for our OK
For a device that spites the moon.
Your timing is inopportune.
We approved one of these yesterday
For Tycho Brahe.
Don't go away mad.
Don't even go away
As we would like for you to be
Our fiancée.

Who's the fairest of them all?
His IQ's off the charts,
He puts horses before carts,
He walked before he could crawl.
Don't recall?
It ain't y'all.

Tell us something we don't know.
Good luck with that since we're all-knowing.
Tout-puissant as well, yet easygoing.
Not just your average Joe.
Oh, no.
Strummin' *Non je ne regrette rien*
On the old banjo.

You have wasted, it would seem, our time.
You've naught to wow the marketplace,
Nor procure for you our grace,
Nor win pardon for your crime.
So you'll do time.

Before you do, though—wait, don't go yet, listen:
We are out of rhyme and with
The rent due we just wondered, Buddy,
Can you spare a dime?

Moirai

Who
by the light of the bonfire of maps
of the world, of passports, love letters,
last wills and testaments, documents
proving our birth, our leatherbound,
autographed novels, our private edition
French cooking and Asian home remedy
books, has brought us here naked
and sunburnt with sores that won't close
on the balls and the heels of our feet
to applaud every sentence of some
donkey's three-hours-and-counting
inaugural speech?

What
did we do in our previous life
to arrive upside down in the
HOV lane of a cul-de-sac
running on empty and revving
in red with the cops in pursuit
and our Hankooks all flat
right smack dab at the end
of the Interstate?

When
in the course of human descent
from the right of free speech
to forbidden dissent,
from free-love caprice
to the Days of Rogation
when steering by stars
yields to echolocation
should every debate about
scallions or chives be settled
with bludgeons and axes
and knives?

Where
there be dragons you scholars
prepare for the knock on the
door, the command to forswear
your belief in the rightness of
swine before pearls. Salute, click
your heels when the new flag unfurls;
Spit out your chewing gum, empty
your locker. *Arbeit macht frei*
by injection has proven to be
taken just before bedtime a
safe and effective tax-free
beta blocker when chased with
unsweetened weak tea.

Why
can't we just get along
in the smothering soot of the bong,
the oil-slickened sea, the ten parts
per million of sulfur dioxide we
can't even smell, touch, or see?
No clue? I'm with you, 'cause it
sure beats the hell out of me.

Apologia

Words
Cannot express the depth of our
Regret and so we will not splutter
Oops, so sorry, our mistake.
Instead, we wear for you our hangdog look
And make a contribution in your name
To Alms-Dot-Org or any other philanthropic
Outfit of your choice. As well, we've sent
Off to the Times a self-condemning op-ed piece.
Are we square now? No, how could we be
In light of the enormity
Of our offense?

Although
Of course
Offense was not intended.
What we did was driven
By the purest of intent.
Although
Of course
That does not mitigate in
Any way our guilt.

Still,
However, might you not admit
That now, pursuant to our act,
There is a certain benefit?
You can't pretend your life
Before that moment was suffused with
Love and light.
All right,
There was a bit of each but
For the most part you were hip-
Bone-deep in muck.

Correction:
You had sunk up to your neck so
Thank your lucky charms that we
Showed up with block and tackle
And that for a modest fee we winched
You out. You might say therefore that
you owe to us your life.
But don't.
The hero's chapeau sits uneasily on our head,
And there are those out there who'd kill
To see the golden idol dead.
Assassination's what we dread.
It's not the villains whom
The hanging judge attaints:
It's the saints.

Audition

I'm the one responsible
Because I built it. Thus I'll take
The blame, though of malign intent
I'm innocent.

My object was to rid the world
Of you-know-what. Thus unencumbered
We'd be free to jive and wail on days both odd
And even numbered.

Too long had we malingered post-op
Grousing and complaining of
Persistent pain where had been placed
The stent.

We'd let ourselves grow fat
Consuming nickel-plated, underage, and
Oversalted this-and-that, seduced
Less by the taste than by the scent.

Far was from me the thought that I
Could forge a golden spike to wed
The rails of accolade and calumny;
I was an empty suit, a talking head,
Ill-born to put to bed

The vicious rumors that had killed
The golden geese. That said, when
Duty calls I answer to my queen.
I am in thrall to naked power;
Vassal to Her Grace; a slave to
Beauty; Chattel of the Winged
Victory of Samothrace.

And thus and therefore I do not
Protest the verdict of the justices
Of Captain Kangaroo's imperial
Court, although I must point out
That while it was the verdict of
The major part there was that one
Vote of dissent. I hope it isn't
Too too cold the place where
He or she has now been sent.

In closing let me cry aloud that
Might makes right and whisper
With my dying breath that it's
A far, far better thing I do than
I have ever done
And all of that.

I'm finished.
Did you like it?
I can do it to the tune of Dixie
Or no, no, no, wait, don't tell me,
You'd prefer it sotto voce.
Or no, maybe I should smile more.
God, I need this job,
My unemployment's
Gone. In spite
Of that if I just
Get this job
I'll be all right.

Diddly

They had their chance,
They could've been heroes,
Could've been aces, studs,
Showered, if not in champagne,
Then beer. Oh say, can you see
Based on bloodline alone what
They could have and should have
But leastways the last time I checked
Just ain't turned out to be?

Stymied by cognitive cowboys,
Trolled by the chelated sophists
Of Rangoon-on-Tyne, their
Toothpicked, saliva-slick, corn-
Fed amygdalas shivered their timbers
In three-quarter time.
What is sad is that although they tried
All the moon-June and hells-bells
Contraptions, by end of the day
They were not only failing to thrive
But also to rhyme.

What happened, I'm guessing, is
They stubbed their great toes and
Too proud to beg sucked it up
'Til the nails first turned black
And then green.
Only then (much too late)
They applied sticking wickets
Of two parts mojito and four
Of the Sabin vaccine, as opposed
To what Rx-dot-com recommends
Which is twenty-five Milk Duds
Dissolved in a dram of benzene.

Belles of the balls in auld lang syne,
Beaux in their brilliantine,
They're seldom heard from these days,
Seldom seen.
All there is to remember them by
Is the whiff of their souls in the air
Now so faint as to make us suspect
That for all of this time they were not really here
And before that were not even there.

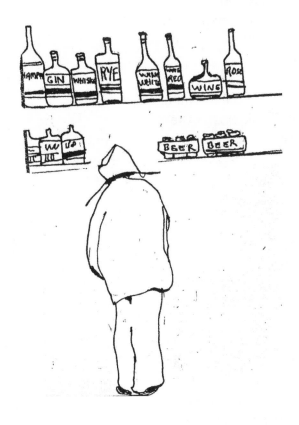

Felon

There must be clues to what occurred,
If it occurred
At all.

There would be finger
Printing on the Mars
Bar; strands of sugared
Angel's hair; teeth wrenched
Loose and scattered on the
Frozen tundra; echoes of a
Long-ago state fair.

Indeed, right there:
The Ghost Of Christmas Present,
Leg demurely over leg in that
Reclining chair.

But of course the moment
That you look, it isn't there
Because you change
The crime scene when
You catch its eye and
In that moment you become
The crime instead:
Perp walking,
Hands bound,
Car door opens,
Watch your head.

Chin up, inside the big house
You'll be warmly clothed
And more or less
Well-fed. To while away
The years sing lieder or
Recite the alphabet from

A to Zed or if you're really
Going mad say very loudly
To your cellmate all the things
That really are much better
Left unsaid.

That done, it will be time
To whisper prayers for my
Forgiveness as you kneel,
Hands clasped, beside what
No one would describe as
Your fourposter downy-
Pillowed featherbed.

Hand on the Constitution now:
Give me this day, and all the days,
Your fresh-baked, poppy-seeded
Daily bread.

Despots

It was doggerel, the sappy little poem
or, more aptly put, the limerick
which we'd dashed off in seven
seconds flat: Our way of saying—thanks?
Yes, thanks, why not, for all they do for us.
Without them we could not, we let them think, exist.
Reciting such godawful we won't even call it
verse brought up the bile into our throat but they
like little half-wit schoolkids being read some
nursery rhyme from Mother Goose sat glassy-
eyed, their elbows on the banquet table, rapt.

Our betrothed and we repaired to
separate rooms that night, tradition
dictates that, and next day bright and early
we were standing face-to-face, you now
may kiss the Holy Book, I do, I do,
and all of that. Out there they sat,
some with, some without hats,
all haunch-to-haunch and sheening
in the monstrous August heat;
some had passed out.

Most heads of state like us will fly to
islands for their wedding night but
we did not, we like to show the common
touch, we took the bridal suite atop the down-
town Marriott. Below our window
they all stood unmindful of the storm
and soot, their lonely eyes imploring
us to step out with our champagne
flutes, post-coital cigarettes between our
milky lips. We did not, and indeed wished
not to disappoint.

Their guns, we now suspect in perfect
twenty-twenty retrospect, were cached
already in their belts. We therefore stood
like target figures, two unwitting ducks
in blissful ignorance and when we kissed
applause broke out; we nodded
in acknowledgement.

Whatever would become of them,
we sometimes wondered, if one day
we happened to depart? Would they
evaporate?

Amusing thought, though we would never
go, of course, by choice at any rate.
They wouldn't stand a snowflake's
odds in Hell alone, some scourge
would wipe them out, nine-tenths of them
at least, the sickest, weakest of the lot.
And thus survive the fit.

Survival, ah, we know a thing or two
of that. The Marriott today, ironically
enough, serves as their revolutionary
operations base. Their quaint devices
which they use to gather so-called truth,
hand-powered thumbscrew iron maiden and
the rack, more medieval you could say than
quaint, are in the kitchen in the basement.
They've extracted nothing of the slightest
consequence from us.

We keep in mind that *tout est pour le mieux,*
and that *arbeit macht frei* (a proven fact),
lest we or anyone forget that this world
out of all the worlds that could or might
exist, is certainly the best. Put that into

your pipe. We taught them that and now,
the hour so late, the moon descended
down the sewer out of earthly sight,
we bid them all the sweetest
of the sweetest dreams
goodnight.

Black Site

The guards awakened us, we'd barely
gone to sleep, they strip-searched first
the women then the rest of us (trim off the
limp discolored outer leaves of late-picked
artichokes), but Frank refused to shed his
boxer shorts, not smart, he paid the price
for his recalcitrance.

WHAT HAVE YOU DONE TONIGHT?
WHO HAVE YOU SEEN?
WHERE DID YOU MEET?
WHAT DID YOU TALK ABOUT?

We shrugged, stayed mute,
(The artichoke grows wild in
shallow water, in canoes is
how you harvest it, our good friend
Nancy Sheffer says to trim the stalk,
cut off the limp discolored outer
such and such.)

IF YOU NAME NAMES
THEN YOU ARE FREE GO.

By our silence we said no,
we won't give up our friends,
that's not what good friends do.
Then as expected we were hit with
pipes, my kneecap shattered with
one blow. Just think, I thought,
if I just shouted:

Nancy Sheffer!
She's the one we met!
Here is what we talked about!

then all the blows would stop
and we would be released.
(The way to teach your cockatiel to
play with toys is play with them
yourself thereby to show your
feathered friend the way to
merry-make.) But we were
beaten every hour all that night
and all the rest of that whole week.
(A cockatiel needs time to feel at home
in human space just as, if we were birds,
we likewise would.) Now badly beaten Frank
is in a catatonic state. We do not dare to make
the sound that we would make
if we were fools enough
to weep.

(You want a good read pick up
Nancy Sheffer's book about the
artichokes of New York State.) Frank
sprawls there on his back and looks
just like a cat run over by a Mack
truck. (Once a bird's chicks fledge
they're all pushed out and some
fly free and some are mauled by
catatonic cats in heat all howling
all the night trim off the outer part
it's blackened now and much too limp
to eat with pipes our best friend Nancy
Sheffer noted in her pioneering book.)

WHAT HAVE YOU DONE?
WHO HAVE YOU SEEN?
WHAT WAS THE SUBJECT OF YOUR CHAT?

We play dumb: *What chat?*
And then the pipes, the pipes,
she wrote.

Potlatch

Oaken dinner table linen napkins linen
tablecloth the sprays of jonquils asters
hyacinths the china mirrorlike so that
the honored dinner guests can see
their face in it, the *boeuf en daube* the
slightly pink *gigot d'agneau* the dead-
and-gone-to-heaven *mousse au chocolat.*
But wait, these guests were promised Native
dishes Utes Paiutes the ones who live on buttes
the Hopi Arikara Ponca Pima Crow Nez Perce.
Ahem, intones the leader of the more than
somewhat disappointed day-tripping
dinner group, we'll have exactly what
those Nez Perce kill and skin and eat
or else we want our money back
each C-note ponied up
for what was billed as
Amerindian Living History Night.
But wait, what's this?
Behold the light fantastic tripping
of the Red Man and his troupe:
Hee-ah-hah, hee-ah-hah,
hey-na-na-ho.
Now that's more like it, that's the ticket,
kiva tipi tom-toms arrowheads an eagle
feather clenched between the teeth
though still the guests regret their suppers
at a hundred bucks a plate weren't just
a tad more tribal-like, it would have
made the whole shebang complete.
Ah well, the paying patrons think,
it's petty at this point to bitch,
there will be time anon
for such complaints.
For now they'll just sit back, light up
their favorite cigarettes and give

their digestifs a sip because the
shaman's just about
to start his schtick:
The world! The stars!
he yelps.
The plants! The sphere of death
encircling life, the howling growling
wolf! Sir Black Elk speaks!
The shaman's native tongue is not
the dinner guests' and so his yelps
alas are to their tone-deaf
Indo-European inner ears
just gibberish.
The leathery crone who sits cross-
legged to the shaman's right translates:
The moon! The starry firmament!
The diners fail to see the point and yet the hairs
uprise upon their necks as now they see the
shaman evanesce, his place assumed
by porpoises and goats and whales
and bears who swipe up salmon
made of burning wood.
Alarmed, those armed amongst the guests
raise up their blunderbusses to protect
their ladyfolk now fearing for their
little lives but fear is moot because
the fauna are just native troupers
garbed in hides and fur of forest beasts
in just the way that all these palefaced men
at table both left-leaning and
conservative alike are sporting
cufflinked shirts of silk beneath
their pinstriped English or Italian suits.
One natty gent is so impressed
he weeps his toes are tingling
eyes are wet he feels Great Spirit
in his gurgling gut.

Hee-hah!
he shouts and everyone shuts up.
Oh God, he thinks. I've put
my foot in it.
So sorry!
he cries out.
I just forgot myself I got so damned
deep into it. Proceed! Don't stop!
And do feel free to pierce
my tongue with stingray
spine should I be rude
once more and interrupt.
That's how you folks appease
your gods, correct? By letting blood
and cinching up your wampum belt?
I know, I've seen the films,
I've read the books.
Don't stop the show
on my account.
And so, thank God, they don't,
although it seems they've finished
with the dancing part and now
they want to talk.
Dear friends, the dancing
we've just done for your
enlightenment (the crone again
translates) *is how we used to dance*
in times of old when we were
blind to Christ.
Beg pardon? You were blind to who?
the dinner guests inquire. Say what?
But now the Good Lord pities us
and sends his One Begotten Son.
We know this thanks to you.
We've seen the film, we've read the book
which you have kindly, very kindly given us.
Film? What film?

"The Greatest Story Ever Told"
or something of that sort.
What book?
The one that's bound in black with
words in gold leaf on the front.
Oh, that book.
Yes, the Good Book as you call it.
Well, all right, if you insist.
A good read, granted, but
it puts us right to sleep.
Did we say that?
Hail Mary full of grace
don't tell our priest.
It is our honor here tonight to see
so many brothers who are white,
so many sisters also, blue-eyed,
teeth so starry bright.
We want you to appreciate
that we have been so long
benighted in the dark. Now
you have brought us light
and taught us what is right.
Did you enjoy your supper
plates? We made you what
we understand
you like.
No wait, that's back-
wards, we came here to
savor what you native gals
and fellows eat to wit
tripe soup and roasted
tail of antelope blue corn
which you call maize and
for dessert perhaps a button
of peyote for an extra
special treat. For God's sake
we can get our shake and fries

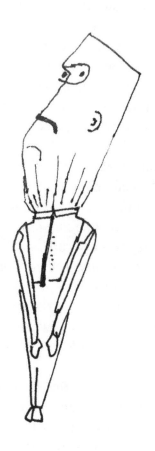

at drive-in windows any given
day or night.
*We do not understand your
tongue and therefore what
you say cannot be understood.
Now take:*
Take what?
The shaman sheds his bear or bison suit
(the guests cannot tell which)
he's naked underneath.
He drops the hirsute garment at their feet.
Now take
he then repeats.
The guests in consternation
shake their heads:
Beg pardon, we cannot.
Oh yes you can,
the crone instructs,
In fact you must.
The guests hold firm explaining that
though once upon a time they sashayed
blithely in their minks and foxes
to their charity events
they now eschew on ethical
grounds the wearing of the pelts
of wild and woolly beasts.
And ethics quite aside, they add,
the legal question rises here,
to wit:
This whaddyacallit custom . . . ?
Potlatch.
Potlatch, right. It's outlawed now,
we thought, this giving of your wealth
to bind the one who takes it
to reciprocate.
We don't care
the crone shoots back

if it was outlawed
or was not by any act
of civil government.
As of now we answer not to
legislators or to potentates.
As of now we answer only to
A Greater Power Higher Up.
Capiche?
She points to heaven.
She is right
the shaman states.
His wish is our Commandment
and His wish of late is that
we discontinue ancient rites
such as this potlatch business
which He warns will leave us
in a bankrupt state.
Henceforth we will
nevermore engage in it.
This show tonight is our
farewell performance
so to speak
and you few have the luck
to witness it and not just that
but also to participate.
The shaman shakes the bear or bison hide
and from the fur a waft of motes emits
to swirl and settle on the china plates.
Next he flings the skin right
in the faces of the guests
who shrink from it.
Take it!
They do not.
Goddamnit, take!
There is spittle, more like
froth upon the shaman's lip.
Just put the damn thing on,

the crone instructs the fuddled group.
What gift,
they ask her, can we offer
in return that matches this?
You offered it already
when you offered Jesus—
—yes, yes, Christ. You should
have tossed him back.
(It shocks to hear the near-
apostasy that spews sometimes
from pious persons' traps.)
Oh what the hell let's get
this over with they start
to step into the belly of
the shaggy beast.
No stop!
the crone protests.
You must undress.
Day-tripping folks like these
are shy, they are reluctant at the gym
post-hot yoga or after lifting weights
to shower sans their bathing suits.
But they accede to her request.
A moment later they've in effect
become the bear or bison
doesn't matter which they're
grunting growling in a sad attempt
to make the noises of whatever sort
a forest creature makes
pathetic really but of course
they are the urban and suburban type
whose knowledge of their furred and
feathered friends derives from
cartoons on TV and Golden Books.
The shaman now is poking through
the clothes his guests have shed
he takes a fancy to a French cuffed

shirt and a pair of cuff links gold
inlaid with Tanzanite
and as well a navy worsted
pinstriped suit and when he
dons these muftis lo behold
they are a perfect fit.
He touches now his forehead then his gut
then both his shoulders, the familiar
signing with the cross
whole bit.
In nomine Patris
and all that.
Be fruitful and go forth until
a millionfold you have
multiplied the number
of your folk.
Sure thing, got that,
the guests retort with edge as if
by now they've had enough
of burlesquing a hooved
or four-pawed brute.
Fun is fun
we've learned our lesson
now though we want out.
The crone unzips the carcass and they
tumble in their rashy nakedness
from the feral blackness into light.
First thing they say:
Now how about we get
our panties and our pinstripes back?
I am afraid,
the crone relates,
it is too late for that
just as the shaman strikes
a match and touches flame
to all the classic well-bred fabric
on his back:

He's instantly ablaze from
head to foot recalling Buddhist
monks in old Saigon whose
mode of protest was to
sit down in a public park amidst
the lunchtime strollers and
self-immolate.
This shaman's just a copycat.
Now you
he tells the guests
as he incinerates.
Us?
the guests reply.
No, thank you,
we will die in our pajamas
in our duvet
in our own good time
surrounded by our spouse
and kids in our fourposter bed.
You think the world should end in fire;
we do not.
We're cold-blooded
much as we may envy those
who like it hot.
The crone shoots them
a killer look.
If that's the way you want it, fine,
she barks,
but you've been warned
so all that I can say to you
is never turn the other cheek
and if you do
good luck.
She hawks up something in her throat
but doesn't spit
then whistling while she works
she whisk-brooms up the ashes

of the former chief
within the char of which
a cuff link glints.
Beg pardon ma'am,
the leader of the
pilgrim group calls out on seeing
what the crone is picking from the soot.
That's mine I think.
You mean,
she says,
this hunk of scrap?
This fool's gold chunk,
she says,
of marcasite?
It's eighteen karat gold,
he claims,
with my initials etched on it
and I would like so much
to have it back.
Too late,
the crone retorts,
and swallows it.

$$f/8$$

Hegira

The old blue liner, hawser-
shackled, champs to put
to sea (her farewell crossing).

In the aft lounge we command
our third Old Fashioneds, whiskey
sours, daiquiris.

The dockhands out there
on the Quai de Normandie
can barely stand against the force-
eight gale. One like a maple leaf
is borne aloft then pitches headlong
back to concrete earth. A dockhand
is a hardy chap so he'll be fine,
we all agree.

And now we're told that what was
force-eight has become a force-nine gale
and so the harbor pilot tells the captain
that we cannot sail, at least not presently.

The hell we can't! our captain hoots.
The wind's died down to summer breeze
velocity! Don't you see that slack Tricolore?
How bat-blind can you be?

The pilot, stung, relents. He merely is a pilot
whereas Captain Krug commanded gunboats
and was honored with the Silver Laurel Wreath
surmounted by the Spangled Crown for his
Conspicuous Gallantry. (It's pinned to his
lapel for all to see.)

Our lines are thus cast off until
the last which hitches, snags, and tangles

on the cleat and as a sudden ten-force gust broad-
sides the ship and shoves us past the tugs' restraint,
that cable, rubber-banding, breaks and then the
length that's still land-fast snaps back and
strikes the same poor dockhand
with result that right leg
disunites from hip.

On learning of this sad event we
all forgo our final drink, deciding
that the money would be better spent
on this now single-legged gent,
and knowing that prosthesis costs
a pretty cent the jolly Texan in our
group (surprisingly a Democrat)
bares his head suggesting that
we pass the cowboy hat.

We're in New York by end of week,
greeted there with water cannons,
fireworks, and every kind of pomp
and circumstance befitting this blue-
blooded dame's retirement.
A perfect crossing and a perfect
welcome home salute!

But now goodnight, my queen, until
next time we see you in the breaker's
yard a fifty-thousand-ton agglomerate
of metal scrap.

But let us take your picture as you are
now and we'll send it to that dockhand
back in France as a memento of a
voyage for the ages on a ship
to end all ships.

Conjugation

I
sip witch hazel so each bite of bony,
leathered meat is moistened just enough
to make a paste. It's damn hard work.
You want a cushy job? A sinecure?
Don't volunteer to masticate.

You
start the war by hurling paving stones
and then you sue for peace on earth
good will toward men from Mars and
Venus take the hindmost sudden
deathly overtime.

She/He
pitches perfect gamesmanship to win
the Senate seat and then wakes up to find
that she/he is afloat in Hudson's Bay
in Henry Hudson's boat: All hands
on Decalogue; God save the Pentateuch.

We
hold these troops to be self-evidently
no one gave a thought to mission creep,
now full five fathom deep Our Father
lies right through his sharp-filed cuspids
and his wisdom teeth.

You,
and I mean all of you beloved dearly
sounding eerily like a Proud Boy toying
with a flat foot floogie with a
floy me to the moon: Floy joy,
floy doy, oy vey, oh boy.

They
shouted: Hey, c'mon, get happy,
chase the refugees away,
forget your troubles, hallelujah,
prices slashed, no-interest loans
on Judgment Day.

Songbird

So what's your take, are they
all right? Their house is dark
and when I call they don't
pick up. Their dog howled all
last night, their lawn is flooded as
the sprinkler has been on all week.
That siren in the middle of last night,
the hook-and-ladder and the squad car
and the ambulance, what were they about?
I asked the medics what the hell was up.
Who wants to know, they said.

As neighbors they
were quite all right although they
borrowed sugar daily by the cup,
played Connie Francis records.
I complained, they didn't stop. As well,
the constant clicking of their fingers
on their keyboards kept me up at night.
And their damn pup bit my foot,
drew blood, and I got rabies 'cause
I don't believe in vaccination shots.

That said, they
were courageous, writing what they wrote
and knowing who would not be pleased
when it appeared in print. Their current
disappearance is, no doubt, because they
exercised their right of what is called
free speech. I tried what they tried once
and that's why now you see me
walking with a limp.

I know, you thought that I'd absconded
on a month-long pleasure trip, as per the
press report. Ha-ha, if that was pleasure
then I don't know what's a junket all
expenses paid with tips included to
a desert penal camp.
(I know whereof I speak.)

Hello? You there?
Say something.
What's that sound?
Is that a beep?
Are you recording?
So am I.
We'll see whose tape
gets to the regulators first.

Collateral

The news of the shooting was page one.
My first thought was it might be you.
The person shot, I mean.
Of course you weren't the shooter,
You don't even own a gun,
Whereas I own a few.

If I may ask, when it happened
Where were you?
Safe at home, I pray.
Not within a day's drive of the deadly scene.
Tell me you were barricaded in your bungalow,
Or on the roof, above the fray.
Don't tell me you were in the line of fire.
I won't believe you anyway.

No, you're too smart to venture out alone
To where the pavement ends, too shy
To ask directions which in any case you
Would ignore. Instead you shelter in your
Ignorance, hug the as-yet unpolluted shore
As you will do, if not forever, then, with luck,
For just a few days more.

Unless since last we talked you've grown a spine,
And now eat peaches on a dare, and roll the
Bottoms of your trousers high exposing knee
And, if you've had your cocktail, also thigh
To persons well outside the wire where you
Have wandered at your mortal peril, now
An easy target for the Brownings on the rooftops
And the Walthers driving by who might not
Know your name but have no doubt that
You are ripe to die.

If that was you appearing in my sights that day,
Well, it was business, nothing personal,
Is all that I can say.

Entente

You would like to shoot a man.
You say it, thumbs in belt loops,
one foot rightward, one foot straight ahead.

You say it not as a statesman would.
You are no statesman. I am a statesman.
and what I think you mean is much,
much better left unsaid.

Have I thought what you are thinking,
just not said it?
Yes and no. I have no answer
save for that and that is more
already than I should have said.

The question that's more apt is
in doing what I did, or did not,
did I enjoy it?

Yet more apt than that is
what disposed me to the act?
Or, better said, what inspired it?

Oh, you say, those questions
miss the point. The best
if not the only question isn't
have I shot but
have I been shot at?

You, at sunrise, are the one
to answer that.

Prime Mover

The lightning struck,
The oak exploded,
Sherwood Forest burned
Because you pared your thumbnail,
So it's all on you.

The plates slip-slid, the wave
Arose and broke, the village was
Engulfed and swept to sea
By virtue of your playing *My Gal Sal*
On your kazoo.

You threw fastballs 'stead of curves
And consequently we're afflicted
With a novel strain of Spanish flu.

You insist you're not to blame
For these catastrophes. You're not
The butterfly who flaps his wings
And causes hurricanes.

Oh, you're not?
Sez who?

Stasi

Be thankful that your name
is not my name.
My name is Buster Blue.
If that was your name then tonight
you'd hear the car wheels on the gravel
then the porch would creak beneath their boots
and then they'd knock.

If your name were Buster Blue (pray God
it's not) then you'd have scratched it off
your mailbox; all your windows you'd
have boarded up to make them think
that you no longer lived here.
They would pass you by (let's hope) and
nail some other fellow with your name
a little farther down the block.

Poor Buster Blue who minus all malign
intent let slip a word that is proscribed
in their new proper usage book; thus now
the bounty on his head.
It's hard to fathom why the mouthing
of a common preposition would be cause
for them to want him dead but it is not
for us to fathom; it's for us to keep
our noses to the grindstone and our eyes
upon the road ahead.

Poor Buster Blue but likewise poor poor
me and you and all the ninety-seven other
innocents in town who answer to this name
and thus are bound by nominal association
as per decree to bear in kind the blame.

So when they find you tell them you are
Wolfgang Mozart or Francisco Franco
although that will do no good because
I'll know you just the same.

The Proud and Randy Fellows

Of the proud and randy fellows
Four came running, running, running
From the clinic where they'd gone
To have their chronic laughter fixed.
Chew this, the doctor said.
They did and felt much worse,
And then an X-ray showed they
Had a stage four this or that which
Had been symptomless and
Therefore never diagnosed.
Next time, the doctor lectured,
You'll remember that a sip of wine
Dissolves the host.

Of the proud and randy fellows
Three came tumbling, tumbling, tumbling
Down to caverns lightless, airless, there
To see descending bachelors strip
Their new brides bare upon the
Even and uneven stair.

Of the proud and randy fellows
Two came shucking, shucking, shucking
Undergarments, plucking graying chestal
Curls, thus scattering the girls.
Raise hand to forehead as
The grand old flag unfurls.

Of the proud and randy fellows
One came lying, lying, lying,
Said he wasn't really dying, just reclining
For a beat, all while from every unhealed
Wound his fluids ran like maple sap.
Come closer, cup your ear, and
You shall hear his heartstring snap.

So when you want to run, just don't.
Your tumbling days are done, you hope.
And if you have to shuck, don't lie
Unless a Cardinal with a pocketful
Of rye Indulgences
Is standing by.

Guest Services Directory

A cleaning fee tra la tra lee
will be charged to thee
for smoking in this hostelry
it will be charged, as Bobby
Sox would say, with glee.
Want ice? Hot tea? A pinch between
the cheek and gummy bear and grin it,
checkout starts at ten to six
when Mistah Kurtz performs his Trixie
Dixie Cups size D.

If flicker flares and conflagrates:
Stay calm, breathe deeply, curse your
fates then pull the fifty shades of grey-
beard looney tunes the Captain
Hook and ladder's on the way
thanks be to Pontius piloting the DC-
3-peat rhyming triplets all begot
back in the day by E. Saint V.
Millay.

On the chance your Shih Tzu
shitz upon the carpet you will
payment made by check is
subject to at least ten years' delay.
Room key, doom key, disco boom key,
bellboy band will play the hits no
runs no airhead plumber's friendly
fireman puts a mint upon your
pillbox whether you're a he
or she.

Wi-fi by the bye is free
love and we disallow, nay,
proselytize for prickly polyamory.
Yer HBOberammergau, yer
Fox Noose Flixnet Cooking
Charnel Food Networkers
of the World United Airline
airport shuttlecocking sir or madam
my way or the high macadam
two-lane bricktop Mary Badham
scouts locations for the bed and
breakage penalty.

We be, as you surmised,
smoke-freebie buffet business
center do not enter, as a renter
you forego all rights to suckle
at the teat of Pooh Bear's
female progeny.

Time to squint and
read the fine prince
consort *damen herren*
belles and buoy
ratatouille Huey Dewey
Lewy Body fronto-tempura
norimachiavelli
what's on telly
sing a song of
old New Delhi
grease the skids with
K-Y Jelly.
Go to helly.
What's that smelly?
Dead raccoon or dope?

The former you'd better hope:
We garrot you stoners with rope
all on orders from
everyone's best friend
the Pontiff of Potpourri
Monsieur Le Pope
sitting pretty in Her Holy See.
So pretty, now don't you agree?
Say *oui*.
Don't dare utter nope.
No toothpaste? Use soap.
Fresh clean out of dope?
Can't cope?
Here's hope:
The desk clerk sells kisses
but won't let you grope
past her knee.
One last plea:
Just don't use the bidet to pee.

$f/16$

Lost At Sea

Our body is a pebble and a flat one,
pancake-like. More precisely, we are
discus-shaped, and let's be frank, we are
not so much a pebble as a stone.
No, stop right there: We are a rock!

Now from the endless shingle he, the boy,
the flaxen-head, selects us from the trillions
upon trillions of our sort, then flings us out
but inexpertly such that we do not go hop-
and-skipping o'er the drink, a lily pad sprung
to existence every time that we alight, one
larger than the next until in their eventual
diminishment they imply
a vanishing point.

No, we instead are canted as we arc
and meet the water edgewise,
disappearing like a dime
into a slot.

So much for that.

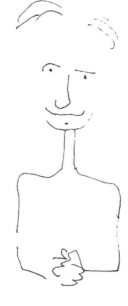

Laureate

We were born to bleacher bums,
Kill The Ump! their battle cry.
Breast-fed on the National Past
Time 'til the age of reason when
we pinch-hit, reached first base
on shortstop's error, second on a
fielder's choice, and third we don't
know how or why, and then we
made it home by bedtime on a
passed ball with the birdies
in the grandstand cheeping
What a Guy.

Elected to the Hall of Fame
(first-rounder) we protested
our unworthiness:
We're an MVP? My eye!
They said: *You either take*
this honor gratefully,
or die.

No-brainer that one since uneasy lies
a Hall of Fame unfit crowned head
and so we chose the latter option. Now
we meet our maker conscience clear,
albeit dead.

Feedlot

We were born belowdecks;
Swaddled in a sheltering sky;
Baptized in a mill race
By a man with a plan to turn water to beer
Who was wandering by.

We grew teeth then lost them;
Were granted a shiny new pair;
Discovered our best friend
Named My Little Margie in fact
Wasn't there.

We were instructed in thuggery;
Coached in the art of the steal;
Counseled at bedtime by working girls
Studying hard in the daytime to earn
The Good Housekeeping Seal.

We were plumped with savoy truffles,
Fattened with alphabet stew:
Raised up for slaughter. Why didn't
We run for our lives? Well, the answer
To that is whate'er would become of us
We never knew.

Misfit

Our presence was more
Suffered than enjoyed,
The papers said.
At least that's what we thought
We read, although we're told our
Name did not appear in print.

And yet, and yet...

Each time we spoke our tongue
Stuck to the mouth of our dry—
No, that is, the roof of our
Dry mouth and so our toast
To bride and groom became
The giant sucking sound
Of jabber going south.

The length of tissue stuck
Onto our shoe sparked gales
Of laughter as we exited the loo;
Our hosts, who'd warmly welcomed
Us, now with their steely eyes
Said Shoo fly, shoo.
(Already they had wished that
We would go away when we mistook
The Bordeaux for the Beaujolais.)

No matter since revenge,
If less than gumdrop sweet,
Is very, very good when
Hosts' McMansions go the way
Of all Norwegian wood.

Obloquy

Fabulations black
As panthers overheard
On Pine and Third, our name
In every other word.
We're innocent! we shout but
Hoots and hisses drown
Our tiny voices out.

Connivance red
As chilis and about
As hot prevents our disentangling
Ten-gauge cord from golden thread;
And so we cannot loose the knot;
Cannot therefore separate the bleeding
From the bled.

Light turns green:
We stop.
Strike three! exclaims the monkey-cop
Now tricycling round and round and
Round the roundabout.
Siddown ya bum yer out.

White as night
Is not, the radon-laden
Basements scrubbed of any hint
Of murder or of prayer. All hail
Our Lord of Fragrant Air.

You, Grand Marshal, mooning
Passersby while spooning from
The sheer blue molten core
Your tasty poultices in the hope
Of waking up tomorrow just a little
Less bedsore.

The contumacious mongrels
Snarling, snarling, snarling
In their dreaded lake of tarry atmosphere.
Oh dear, oh dear,
Forget the libels, slanders, lies:
It's dogs and only dogs we really
Truly fear.

Coup

I wasn't there
At noon
To see, or let alone
To slow, much less to halt
The surge, nor stanch
The flow.

I wasn't there
At one, nor two, nor
Three and so
The fact that such a force had
Breached the dam by then,
Stormed the gates,
Smashed the status quo,
Was, to my own mind,
A fact I didn't know.
So I am not to blame
For our present general state
Of bane and woe.

Had I been there
I'd have been there for, let's say,
An hour or so,
Scant time to raise
Objection, let alone appease
A beast intent on sinking fangs
Into our necks and never
Letting go.
(Its roar was all,
I would have thought,
For show.)

You—*you* were there.
I saw your footprint
In the snow,

Inhaled the scent of your cigar,
Its stub down by the storm drain there
Still aglow.

If it weren't fantastic to
Suppose (the word outrageous
Would much better do),
I'd say the beast
Was you.

The End of the Affair

You are bringing to the boil
a flagrancy of common wisdom,
common inasmuch as it is not
yet written down, has not been
patented, nor has made
the slightest sound,
and thus will only appetize,
if anyone at all,
the Lord and Lady of the Flies.

You grayling you, you northern piker,
shin-deep in the Yukon panning for
a golden rule of thumb that's easy come
and just as easy go while I remain as ever
halfway down between the front lawn and
the molten core, canary of the withered heart
and blackened lung, chirruping
Nevermore.

I am stardust, you are
goldenrod and wisps of
Persian kitty hair and I am
barely breathing, barely daring
to Achoo.
Ach du.
Oh yes, I did love you but
now your feets too big to fit
inside this old brown shoe.

Next Door

Last
week I get this call from Gracie next door
you know Gracie with the missing
pinkie and the limp so Gracie
calls me up says
You too loud
you too loud shut up.
Says it twice.
I say Me who me too loud?
You the loud one, Gracie says, so zip it.
I would zip it, I tell Gracie, if it was
unzipped but hate to break it to ya, ma'am,
I call her ma'am to keep the
convo light, the truth is now
I lost my train of thought
and by the time I get it back
Miss Gracie has hung up.
How I know she lied
that I was loud is on account
of I don't talk.
I make this point
to her fat face I'm at her door
I knock I tell her that
I'm mute.
In that case she pre-
varicates it must be that you
played a tape
and had the volume pumped
cease and desist or I shall phone
the cops Patrolman
Gordy he's my aunt
owes me a favor he will
knock your lights out with his
billy club.
I say is that a threat?

Says Gracie Take it any way
you want.
I say Gracie how I take it is that
you're proposing I should be
your spouse.
And Gracie says
you take it right.
Next thing I do I do
down at the station
house where Gordy the Patrolman
is as well a Justice
of the Peace now
kiss the bride or groom until
the day you're Healthy or in Sickness
You Do Part.
I love you Gracie.
No says Gracie no you don't
shut up I'm filing
for divorce.
So soon? I say. Before
we've had a chance
to fornicate?
That's right.
But why?
'Cause you too loud shut up.
Neighbors. Jeez.
Won't you be
my neighbor Mister
Rogers said well I say
hell with that.

Euphonium

Yesterday morning I woke in Mumbai,
Went walking alone on the streets of Powai,

Espied there a woman in pink and in gold.
I said to her gently: May I be so bold

As to ask you what gives you most joy and most sorrow?
Today? she replied. Or do you mean tomorrow?

Today, ma'am, I answered, is where we should start.
All right, then, she said, from the depths of my heart,

I confess that I bloom on the day of a wedding.
My life then, you see, is all feathers and flowers.
There's music and dancing and wild rapid drumming.

Last night all the women were painted with Mehndi.
My hands here you see are a garden of blossoms:
They mean that my sister the bride will bear children.

Her husband will love her and treat her with kindness.
His mother won't scold her when she burns the roti.
I feel rather sad, though: today will pass quickly.

Tomorrow I won't be in pink and gold finery.
I'll ride in a rickshaw inhaling the diesel
Exhaust from the tailpipes of trucks all marauding

Through traffic that lurches and grinds and the honking
Of horns makes me deaf. I arrive at the office
Still hearing that blaring. I smell of the streets. Now I

Sit at my desk and accept it's all gone now,
My life isn't really a wedding forever,
With clarinets laughing, my heart like a soldier

In step with the drumbeat, the blurting euphonium
Goading the tempo, the fizz of the champagne is
making me witty!
(I'm normally not all the funny, you see.)

But I've had my last sip. My sister's a wife,
After being my very best friend all my life.
In the mornings I'll wake in the bedroom we shared
Abandoned, alone, as if nobody cared,

As if no one remembered her raggedy twin
My pillow my suckling: I'm here lying in

After birthing wee no one (my saddest transgression).
You see me arrayed in postpartum depression,

The virtual kind, since I only gave birth
To the dream of a child, for all that was worth,

Which was nothing and so just as always I mourn
One more pretty pink dream on arrival stillborn.

$$f/32$$

In Common

Suppose that solid truth is Atman;
Beauty then is Brahman.
Now the path to one of them's
The path they have in common.

Truth is Beauty, Beauty Truth,
And Beauty's God as well,
But not a God we worship
For the fear we'll rot in hell

If we skip church, or God forbid,
We take God's name in vain.
Or if like Abel we're preferred
By God and killed by Cain.

Beauty's not a jealous God,
Its quality's not strained.
It droppeth on the place beneath
Just like the gentle rain,

But not from heaven, just from cloud,
Enabling us below
To cultivate our garden plots,
Our roses thus to grow.

A rose is a rose is a rose, it's always
Worthwhile to repeat.
And a rose by any other name
Would surely smell as sweet.

William Stein or Gertrude Shakespeare
Made that observation.
(I'm done for now so you can run
Off to the comfort station.)

Child's Play

Said a poet: If I could
Regain the madness of childhood,
What a fine and lovely madness that would be.
Ah, if I could only live
Near that mad pitch I would give
All the sober wisdom that's accrued in me.

See, the madness of a child
Is pure fancy running wild,
Unrestrained by logic, rules, or dialectic.
Kids are footloose, off the cuff.
They don't fear the kind of stuff
That would make an older person apoplectic.

When you're grown act like a kid;
Don't let the ego rule the id.
As a grownup try to live life to the limit.
Then at the limit just keep going;
Heeling over leads to knowing
When your sail's too full,
And thus how much to trim it.

Pyramid Scheme

Contradictions can be fun,
They're the game both lost and won
Where the bogus can be truer than mere truth.
Yes, at first you are dumbfounded
When you see the square is rounded,
Or you're sweating in the winter in Duluth.

Or at a pyramid's true peak
When you stop to take a leak
You discover there's no surface there to pee on,
'Cause a point's a case in point
Of two lines in space conjoint.
It's a geometric marvel that you're seein'.

What I mean, that point's not physical.
Oh, I know you find it quizzical
That a solid-seeming thing is immaterial.
But now think, is it unpleasant
To consider that the present
Is a moment that's one-time but also serial?

Can't a landlord be a renter?
Or a student be a mentor?
Are all happy celebrants never lamenters?
Some destroyers are inventors.
Some protectors are tormentors.
And each one of us who exits also enters.

Tempus Fugitaboudit

The womb was all comfy and cozy, no doubt.
There's no going back, though, the moment you're out.

The starting gun's fired, the race has begun,
You're out of your cave, now you're under the sun.

The second hand jumps as the clock starts to tick,
Time's done for the dead; just begun for the quick.

How fine it would be if that sweep hand would pause
And time would stand still against all natural laws.

But time waits for no man, nor woman, nor kid.
What you'll do tomorrow it already did.

FAQ

Last Monday entered laughing.
On Tuesday grief came nigh.

On Wednesday I was born again.
So Thursday I could die.

Friday I kissed fame hello,
Then Saturday good-bye.

Now Sunday I have just five questions:
Why? Why? Why? Why? Why?

Ars Gratia

Some pictures are worth a thousand words.
Some only cost a buck-thirty.
True value of course is a factor of whether
The picture is spotless or dirty.

Baited/Switched

We file our claim then on the date
On which we see the real estate
We bought by mortgaging our son and daughter,
That it's not as in the flyer:
'Cause the front yard's muck and mire,
And the back yard's fully six feet underwater.

Pari-mutuel

Life is a gamble that profits the brave
Who gamble on long shots from cradle to grave:

Those horses so lame no one thinks they can run,
Then they bolt from the gate at the sound of the gun,

And soon take the lead which they hold to the wire.
That gun's in your hand now, so aim it and fire

Straight upward of course, so the bullet won't graze
Any spectators. (That's so verboten these days.)

Credo

A brain is the gray matter, neurons, and cells
We can weigh to the last milligram.
A mind is the tune that emotion impels
And allows us to sing: This I Am.

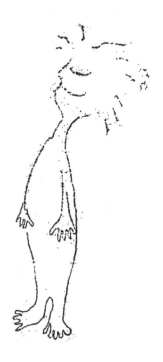

Cakewalk

The mind, we discover, does not live alone
High away in a cold ivory tower.
It dances in step with the flesh and the bone
In a delicate balance of power.

Same Difference

At present I'm feeling euphorically glad;
At the same time I'm somber and blue.
The things that brought happiness now make me sad,
And my craziest fictions are true.

E Pluribus

I promise this, I guarantee
In fair or stormy weather:
That I Am He and You Are She
And We Are All Together.
That's odd, I know, but try to see,
The kid inside me begs:
Just humor me: We're hens and roosters,
And we're all their eggs.

Apt Pupil

Porky Pig owned a parrot named Sue
Whom he taught to say "Oink, oink" on cue.
When the baker came by
To make Porky pork pie,
He mistakenly made parrot stew.

Not OK Cupid

You're in thrall to yellow lunacies,
I'm fogbound in red.

You thaw pack ice with your lighter,
I use salt instead.

We're a pair of honest rhinos,
Clothed as lying sheep.

Wolfing down Miss Riding Hood
While sparing L'il Bo Peep.

Guess we can't get married then,
Each other we'd devour,

You consuming moo shu pork
And I my sweet and sour.

Skill Set

How many rich men
can lie fetal,
eye a camel,
spin a dreidel,
vainly cajole and needlessly wheedle
Dee and Dum the Brothers Tweedle,
draw blood from a knitting needle,
while holding the job of parish beadle?
How many are this type of hero?
Less than zero.

Superguy

What's sorrier
than a receding mullet,
more powerful
than a hidden motive,
able to read long Bildungsromans
both hard and paperbound?
Voir! Haut dans le ciel!
(Pardon my French.)
It's *Übermensch!*

American League Champions

How many LA Angels
can dance on the head of a pinstriped New York Yankee
who asks them to take off
their cleats and dance in
bare feets and after they do
whispers Thankee?
As many as wish
rules the Baseball Commish.

Ask Buffalo Bob

How did Howdy Doody
land the *capo role di tutti
capi* in the final episode of
Downton Abbey wherein
Mister Bluster sleeps
with Sleeping Beauty?
It involved (well, of course)
the severed head of a horse.

All My Loving

Use grounded outlet only,
Then let slip the Tug of War.

Let me be your one and only,
For three minutes, maybe four.

You mean more to me than salad,
I'd be lost without your brains,

And your poncho's not invalid
For protection when it rains.

Is my weekend shining loudly?
Is the mustard running clear?

Is Prince Igor beaming proudly?
Does Jim Beam grin eye to ear?

If your vitals need enhancing,
If your screech-owl's swollen shut,

Come to me for refinancing,
Don't bemoan that bogey putt.

I am here to be your backlog,
I will always speak *ad rem*.

Why is that? A valid question,
And the answer is *Je t'aime*.

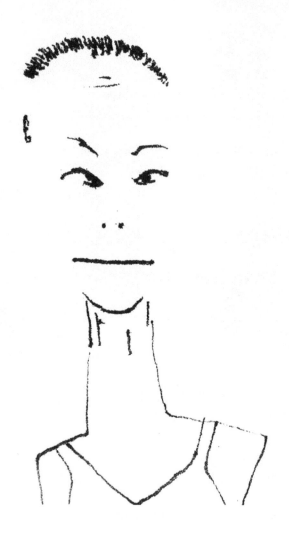

f/64

Ontogeny

Your gray matter's turning to sod;
You once sprinted; you currently plod.
Add to that, your soul aches.
Hey, tough luck, them's the breaks.
If you live past age thirty you're scrod.

Blank Verse Blank

My dad was a master of rhyme
Up until he came down with Alzheim-
ers Disease which I rue
Has afflicted me, too,
For I can't now recall my last line.

About the Author and Contributor

PETER MAECK is a poet, novelist, playwright, and photographer. His narrative poem *Remembrance of Things Present: Making Peace With Dementia* (Shanti Arts, 2017) celebrates his father's brave, good-humored experience with Alzheimer's disease. Peter's novel, *Zänker*, will be published in February 2023. Peter served as US State Department American Cultural Specialist in Tanzania and Morocco. He holds a BA in English from Dartmouth College and an MFA in playwriting from Brandeis University.
—www.petermaeck.com

Peter Maeck's sister **ALEXANDRA MAECK** is a professor of English and a sly and subtle artist with pencil and pen.

SHANTI ARTS

NATURE · ART · SPIRIT

Please visit us online
to browse our entire book
catalog, including poetry
collections and fiction, books
on travel, nature, healing, art,
photography, and more.

Also take a look at our highly
regarded art and literary journal,
Still Point Arts Quarterly, which
may be downloaded for free.

WWW.SHANTIARTS.COM

CPSIA information can be obtained
at www.ICGtesting.com
Printed in the USA
BVHW090125130922
646694BV00004B/27